The Sponsors 12 Step Manual:

A Guide to
Teaching and Learning the
Program of A.A.

A

Get Into Recovery
Production

John E has been active in the recovery field for many years. He is the driving force behind   Get Into Recovery and part of the team at Somerton Lodge. These two things combined lead to a recovery organisation that works together to writes books, training and manuals that also owns Somerton Lodge an alcohol-free hotel and retreat destination on the Isle of Wight, England.

For Anne.

The Sponsors 12 Step Manual:
A Guide to Teaching and Learning the
Program of A.A.

ISBN-978-1475276824
First Edition April 2012.
Revised December 2020

Introduction.

This is not a stand alone guide. For it to be successful you must have access to the Big Book of *Alcoholics Anonymous* and the *12 Steps and 12 Traditions*.

The 12 Steps of Alcoholics Anonymous are broken down into different levels. There are 6 of these, each one is progressively more challenging. If you are already familiar with the 12 Step programme, it may be helpful to read each level before the work is started, there can be a tendency to jump ahead.

Some folks have commented that this book is a bit like going back to school in the way it asks you to complete tasks. I can only apologise but that's the whole point of this learning structure, I'll explain a bit more.

Using Educational theory to teach the 12 Steps.

Whilst on this journey of recovery I was fortunate enough to find myself on many training courses about education and came to believe that there are established educational theories that could be applied to teaching the 12 steps.

I wrote these ideas down, so as to try to become a better sponsor, looking at each step in turn. I applied two of the theories to writing this book. The two pieces of work I studied are easy to digest and make sense to me. The first is written by William Glasser MD who states the following.

How We Learn

10% of what we READ
20% of what we HEAR
30% of what we SEE
50% of what we SEE and HEAR
70% of what is DISCUSSED with OTHERS
80% of what is EXPERIENCED PERSONALLY
95% of what we TEACH TO SOMEONE ELSE

The second piece of work was written by B S Bloom in 1956 and updated by Anderson, L W, & Krathwohl D R (eds.) in 2001. It states that we have different levels of learning and we should master one level before moving on to the next as follows.

Level 1 Remembering	Level 2 Understanding	Level 3 Applying
To recall something to mind.	Knowledge of a particular subject.	To make use of something to achieve a result.

Level 4 Analyzing	Level 5 Evaluating	Level 6 Creating
To examine something in great detail in order to understand it better.	To consider or examine something in order to judge its value, quality or importance.	Give rise to something or make something happen.

I looked at each of the 12 steps and applied these processes to that step in order to produce a progressive learning curve. It is suggested that not all of these categories be mastered by the sponsee before moving on to the next step. That is to say that if a person is really struggling then the sponsor should make the decision to move on and revisit, rather than get stuck.

This guide can be worked through alone, in a group or with a sponsee and sponsor. When the word 'you' is written it can substituted for 'your sponsee, your group or yourself, change the language as appropriate to each situation. Equally, when it says 'learn', 'read' or 'discuss' these should be directed as appropriate. It is always recommended that the 12 Steps are worked with a sponsor, by the nature of the disease of addiction it is very easy to put your own interpretation on any of the materials presented to you.

Some people may find the challenge of testing their own knowledge on the 12 Steps irresistible. If that is you, see if you can answer all of the level 4 questions without referring to the literature.

We are not affiliated with Alcoholics Anonymous or any other 12 step program.

Step 1. "We admitted we were powerless over alcohol - that our lives had become unmanageable."

Remembering Step 1.

The first level of learning is to remember the subject, this is a vital stage in the learning process but may feel a bit pointless or autocratic. The benefits of learning each step so that it can be recalled from memory are tremendous in many ways, not only is it the foundation of further learning but remembering the steps 'off by heart' will lead to the reduction in feelings of isolation. You or your sponsee will feel more at home in a meeting.

Ask him/her to learn Step 1 off by heart.

Understanding Step 1.

For the second level of learning your sponsee must be able to explain the meaning and idea of Step 1. To begin the process of understanding this step your sponsee should take a look at some of the language used. Ask him/her to read the definitions, discuss them and explain them in his/her own words.

There are many definitions of '**admitted**'. Below are some recognised meanings that can be discussed so that the various meanings of the word can be understood. This method will be applied throughout the book so that people understand the words they are using, this is not meant to be patronising but can help with understanding each step at depth.

- Confess to be true or to be the case, typically with reluctance.
- To permit to enter.
- Acknowledge.
- Accept as valid.
- Allow the possibility of.

Discuss the meaning of the word '**admitted**' in Step 1?

There are many descriptions of being '**powerless**'. Below are some dictionary definitions.

- Without ability, influence, or power.
- Lacking strength.
- Being weak and feeble.
- Inability to control the use of alcohol or other drugs by self will.
- The inability to engage in a behavior moderately.

There is one dictionary definition that obviously stands out but is this the only one that is valid? Have a talk about 'powerless' in the context of the step.

The word 'unmanageable' has various meanings. Below are some recognised explanations.

- Difficult or impossible to manage, manipulate, or control.
- Uncontrollable: difficult to solve or alleviate.
- No longer functions successfully.
- Unacceptable consequences of addiction.
- A time in life when a person can no longer function successfully by means of the unaided will.

Again one answer stands out, you may agree, however, that all the definitions are correct. Talk about this word in the context of the step. It is often mentioned that Step 1 is in two parts, now that an understanding of the words used is established let's look at each part of the step and generate some conversation.

'We admitted we were powerless over alcohol.'
Prompt the sponsee to discuss powerlessness over alcohol, do as it says in the Big Book (page 92) and describe some of your own powerless episodes. Remember to keep your examples short, it is your sponsee that needs to demonstrate understanding not you. People can be very good at pretending they understand something when they have no idea what it is

they are pretending to understand, so ensure your sponsee understands it and can identify powerlessness as it relates to him/her.

Working together explore general examples of powerlessness not related to alcohol. Concentrate on the concept of being powerless itself. It will help if you write them down or make bullet points.

'that our lives had become unmanageable.'
Ask your sponsee to describe areas of their own life that are, or have been, out of control. Which of these are as a result of alcohol? Which have been difficult or impossible to manage. Ask them if there any times in their life that were unmanageable when they weren't drinking? Do they know why?

Applying Step 1.
The third level of learning is application. Your sponsee must be able to apply the information learned previously in this step to personal experiences, some prompting questions have been added below to further learning. You may think of more. Ask him/her to write some short paragraphs using the headings below.

- Choose a time when you wanted to control your drinking, how successful were you? What went wrong? i.e. promising to only have 2 drinks at a party.

- Write about a time when you avoided people that weren't drinking, or you hid your drinking from them.
- Choose a period in your life that was unmanageable, e.g. missed appointments or constant lateness and write about it.
- How has drinking affected your self respect or self image?

Discuss why the above questions are related to Step 1.

Analyzing Step 1.

Analyzing is the fourth level of learning. At this level your sponsee will need to examine A.A. writings about powerlessness and unmanageability. This is a great learning opportunity, the work may seem arduous but the benefits are worth the effort.

To complete this section people will need to read **Chapter 3 'More About Alcoholism'**, **'The Doctors Opinion'** and Step 1 in the **'12 Steps and 12 Traditions'**. In order to make the learning process easier during this section a list of questions has been added below. These will help focus the reader on specific points in each chapter. Your sponsee will have to study each chapter to find the answers. There is a companion book to this one that has added to its title 'Workbook Edition' this version follows the same format here but has space for persons to write answers.

Questions on The Doctors Opinion.

- What does the chapter say about the allergy?
- What does the term' a psychic change' mean?
- What effort is required to stay sober?
- Why does Dr Silkworth believe that addiction is not entirely a problem of mental control?
- What are the 5 types of alcoholic that the doctor classifies? Which ones do you identify with?
- What is the 'only relief' suggested?

The next questions are focusing on Chapter 3.

1. What illusion are we pursuing?
2. What delusion has to be smashed?
3. What have we lost?
4. What are you not going to believe and why?
5. List the methods that have been tried in order drink like other people.
6. How can you diagnose yourself?
7. What belief did the man of thirty fall victim to?
8. What is particularly true of women?

9. What examples of Step 1 are highlighted by Jim's story?
10. How does the jay walker story emphasise powerlessness?
11. Read Fred's story and write about what he realised when he regained his ability to think.
12. Why would Fred have to throw out several lifelong conceptions?
13. Finish reading the chapter, what does it say we have no mental defence against?

I have often heard people tell of their inability to relate fully to the stories in this chapter during early recovery. Only to revisit them at a later date and then at that later date really be able to absorb the meanings in full. So perhaps consider revisiting this work at a future date.

Questions on Step 1 in the 12 and 12

20. What does utter defeat enable us to do?
21. What is one of the facts of A.A. life?
22. Why is self confidence no good whatsoever?
23. Why is alcohol a double edged sword?
24. In A.A.'s pioneering time only the most desperate people got well, in the following years this changed to include who? What were they spared?

25. What could we show them that changed their attitude?
26. Why all this insistence that every A.A. must hit a bottom first?
27. How low must your downfall be?

Evaluating Step 1.

The fifth level of learning is evaluation. The task here is to evaluate ideas or materials, judge value quality or importance and learn to see outcomes that could have been different if your sponsee had not been drinking or drugging.

Some questions to answer could be.

- Select a time when you were angry towards someone whilst drinking. What may have been different if you were not drinking? Can you defend your behaviour or can you support the idea that it would have been different if you were sober?

- Compare the difference between stopping drinking and pausing drinking perhaps using the following sentence as an example. "Yeah I stopped for 3 weeks once so I can't be an alcoholic". Pose the question that "was that stopping or just pausing"?

- How does your personality change when you are under the influence of drink or drugs?
- What things have you done to maintain your addiction that you said you would never do?
- Have you ever been in real danger and been so 'out of it' you were completely vulnerable?
- Complete this task: Work out the monetary cost of drinking, produce a spread sheet or graph showing the amount of money spent over the drinking time, it does not have to be exact, just a rough estimate. How much could you have saved?

Creating with Step 1.

The sixth level of learning is the ability to apply what has been learned to creating something new. Create some new discussion points that will highlight powerlessness and unmanageability and can be talked over with a newcomer, this will help to increase understanding.

If you have set a sponsee this task, check the discussion points are appropriate before your sponsee talks to newcomers about this step. Make sure that he/she is ready to complete this part of the learning; you may want to wait until his/her recovery has been firmly established. If working alone you may wish to check your questions with another person before speaking to others.

Step 2. "Came to believe that a power greater than ourselves could restore us to sanity."

Remembering Step 2.

Your sponsee should learn Step 2 off by heart. It is easy to skip this vital level but the benefits of learning the step verbatim are great. This will be the format from now on. Perhaps it could prompt your sponsee to learn all the steps off by heart.

Understanding Step 2.

Your sponsee must be able to explain the meaning and idea of step two. To begin the process of understanding this step ask him/her to take a look at some of the language used, read the definitions, discuss them and explain them in his/her own words.

'**Believe**.' What does believe mean? Some standard definitions follow.

- To have confidence or faith in the truth of.
- To suppose or assume.
- To understand.

As per the same level in the previous step discuss this word in the context of Step 2.

A 'power greater' than ourselves. How do you define power? some definitions are given.

- Might - force - strength -
- Potency - authority - energy
- A person or organization that is strong or influential within a particular context.

So what 'power' is being referred to in Step 2? It might be worth pointing out that in the Big Book it states that a persons higher power can be whatever they choose, just remember that it should be benevolent.

What is meant by the word 'greater'?

- Bigger
- Better
- Higher
- Superior

Consider this word in the context of the step.

Talk about the meanings of 'being 'restored'

- To return to an original or former condition
- To bring back to health, good spirits, etc.
- To reintroduce or re-enforce *to restore discipline.*

- To reconstruct (an extinct animal, former landscape, etc.)

Again a great word for discussion; on its own it is quite clear what the different meanings are but are they right in the context of this step? Perhaps we had better discuss the next word first.

How would you describe **'sanity'**?

- (Psychology) the state of being sane
- Good sense or soundness of judgment
- Free from mental derangement
- Having a sound, healthy mind
- Having or showing reason

A fair few meanings there and often a word that is shied away from. In the context of the step what may it mean? Next we will have a look at the complete meaning of the step and perhaps re-touch on some of the discussion so far. The first part of this step (**'Came to believe'**) stands out as being written in the past tense. Discuss with your sponsee the possible reasons for this.

'a power greater than ourselves.' What is a power greater than ourselves? We often use higher powers but do not believe in them as such. Discuss or list some things that have more power than us. Help the sponsee to recognise that there are many things that are more powerful than us. It does not have to be God. To help understand this, the following teaching story can be used as an ice breaker.

Imagine this conversation between two people.

"Do you believe in a higher power?"
"No"
"If your car was broken would you know how to fix it?"
"No."
"OK so you would take it to the garage? "
"Yes"
"Could that garage then be understood to have greater knowledge than you?"
"Yes" (never was a great talker).
"So in relation to cars the garage is a higher power than you"
"Damn you"

OK a bit of a silly example when we are talking about addiction and a fatal illness, but sometimes people are so stubborn that they refuse point blank to accept that there is any power greater than themselves. This exercise is trying to open people up to possibilities. As long as a Higher Power is 'greater' than the individual, then the only condition is that it should also be loving and caring. Reflect that we often use higher powers but seldom think of them as that.

The final part of the step are the words **'restore us to sanity.'** Explain the mental twist of alcoholism as described in the big book page 92.

In the early days of ones recovery **sanity** may be to confrontational for some, at this point your sponsee only need to grasp that some behaviour has been, or is, illogical, ill advised or just plain crazy... To help consolidate this learning ask the sponsee to try and describe in his/her own words an understanding of sanity and insanity as applied to alcohol (maybe not his/her personal examples but maybe that of others).

Applying Step 2.
Your sponsee must be able to apply the information learned previously in this step to personal experiences. From what he/she has learned already ask him/her to write some short paragraphs using the headings below.

- Choose a time when your behaviour may have been described by **others** as insane.
- If you are behaving sanely then what would that look like?

- Give an example of a higher power helping in a situation that may have been unresolved unless help was obtained.
- Write about a time in your life when you realised that you had to change, did anyone help you?
- Is having a closed mind going to be helpful in your recovery?

How do the above questions relate to this step?

Analyzing Step 2.

At this level your sponsee will need to examine A.A. writings about Step 2.

To complete this section he/she will need to read Chapter 4 We Agnostics and Step 2 in the 12 Steps and 12 Traditions.

In order to assist the learning process easier during this section a list of questions has been added below. These will help focus the reader on specific points in each chapter. The next questions are focusing on Chapter 4.

Chapter 4 We Agnostics

1. What are not always easy alternatives to face? Why?
2. What is our dilemma?
3. What exactly is this book about?

4. What difficulties arise with agnostics?

5. What is it we discover, much to our relief?

6. What is the one short question we need to ask ourselves?

7. What are the 'good reasons' to believe in a power greater than ourselves?

8. On page 52 what should we apply to our human problem, what subjects does the Big Book give as examples?

9. What 'certain kind' of faith does the Big Book say we already have?

10. What idea is deep down in every man woman and child?

11. In the story of the atheist what was the turning point in this mans recovery?

The following are based on Step 2 in the 12 and 12:

12. This chapter identifies 5 different cases of religious belief, what are they?

13. How does a sponsor respond to someone who says he won't believe?

14. What are the three statements.

15. What can we say to someone who has lost faith?

16. What does the intellect have to do to become right sized?

17. Those who are 'disgusted with religion' have substituted negative for positive thinking, what do they have to realize?
18. What is the outstanding characteristic of many an alcoholic?
19. A man full of faith needs to do what?
20. As an example of 'surrender to win' what suggestion may not be endured?

Evaluating Step 2.

Here your sponsee is looking to identify times in his/her own life that could have been considered insane. Ask him/her to describe any personal situations that may have been resolved because of the intervention of a higher power. There are no right or wrong answers. Some questions to answer could be:

- This question is a slight repeat of one asked earlier (Select a time when your own behaviour was insane or even just illogical. Were there any times that someone or something intervened to alter the outcome?) however the main point is to evaluate the idea that, without an intervening higher power, the consequences would have been a lot worse?

- Defend the idea that we cannot restore our sanity on our own and need a higher power in our lives to guide and nurture us back to right thinking.
- What have your previous experiences been with religion? Consider whether this does or does not change your belief of God as you understand him?
- What changes in your **thinking** are necessary to restore you to sanity?
- What changes in your **behaviour** are necessary to restore you to sanity?

Creating with Step 2.

Here your sponsee has to create a list of discussion points that may be discussed with a newcomer that will highlight a power greater than ourselves and how that power can restore us to sanity. This is as important for your sponsee as it is for the newcomer.

If you have set a sponsee this task check the discussion points are appropriate before your sponsee talks to newcomers about this step. Make sure that he/she is ready to complete this part of the learning; you may want to wait until his/her recovery has been firmly established. If working alone you may wish to check your questions with another person before speaking to others.

Step 3. "Made a decision to turn our will and our lives over to the care of God as we understood him."

Remembering Step 3.
Again focusing on that very important level of 'Remembering' ask your sponsee to learn Step 3 and be able to recite it by heart.

Understanding Step 3.
Your sponsee must be able to explain the meaning and idea of Step 3.

To begin the process of understanding this step ask your sponsee to have a look at some of the language used, read the definitions, discuss them and explain them in his/her own words.

What is a **'decision'**?

- The act or process of deciding.
- Making a judgment.
- The act of or need for making up one's mind: This is a difficult decision.
- A resolution - He made a good decision.

What 'decision' are we making in the context of Step 3?

In order to explore **'our will'** further I've chosen to look at it in the context of 'self will'. Explore the meanings of 'self will' given below.

- Stubborn or obstinate refusal to listen to others.
- Pursuing one's own wishes and aims.
- The trait of resolutely controlling your own behaviour.

Does this make sense as applied to Step 3 or does your sponsee see other meanings?

Following on from the above question is the word **'lives'** and it's worth exploring it in the phrase **'our will and our lives'** what does the word **'lives'** mean in this context?

- All of me.
- My behavior and actions.
- 100% of my time.

Spend a little time on this but no too much as it is covered a little later in this section.

What does **'care'** mean?
- Caution in avoiding harm or danger.
- Close attention.
- Upkeep or maintenance.
- Watchful oversight; charge or supervision.

Again in Step 3 how are we understanding this word?

How do we explain 'God?' **Phew!**

- The one Supreme Being, the creator and ruler of the universe.
- One of several deities, especially a male deity presiding over some portion of worldly affairs.
- A supreme being according to some particular conception.
- Life, Truth, love.
- Mind, Soul, Spirit.
- Principle.
- **G**ood **O**rderly **D**ecisions.

Explore some of these meanings, this can be a relaxed conversation with no requirement for anyone to be pushed into believing anything. Their own personal belief will develop over time.

What is the meaning of '**understood'?**

- To perceive the meaning of.
- To be thoroughly familiar with
- To assign a meaning to.
- To have knowledge or background, as on a particular subject.

How does it fit in with Step 3?

Focusing a little harder and perhaps repeating what you may have discussed so far put theses words in more context.

'made a decision'.
Discuss what it means to make a decision. Talk about any decision made that is not followed by action is still only a decision. Here I would like to insert the story I heard about frogs. (Heard in an A.A. meeting)

Three frogs are sitting on a log when two decide to jump off into the water. Question, how many frogs are left on the log?
Answer, three, they only made a decision.

Discuss what it means by **'our will and our lives'** some prompting questions are below.

- Why our will AND our lives, does that mean all of me and everything I do, or can I keep hold of a bit of will power to apply to certain situations?
- Self will, as defined in the Oxford English Dictionary is given as 'Obstinately doing what one wants in spite of the wishes or orders of others'. Discuss the point that we were running

our lives obstinately making decisions based on our own will rather than using the wisdom of others.

'God as we understood him'
Ask your sponsee to discuss his/her understanding of God, remembering that this is his/her own conception not anyone else's.

Applying Step 3.
Your sponsee must be able to apply the information learned previously in this step to personal experiences. From what the sponsee has learned already he/she must write a paragraph demonstrating the ideas and concepts of step 3.

Some questions to answer could be:
- Describe in writing or draw a picture of God as you understand him.
- Write down the characteristics or behaviors of someone running on self will and then the same for someone who has made a decision to run their life according to the will of a beneficial higher power.
- When making a decision about something describe in writing the process that you should follow, especially in early recovery.

How do the above questions relate to this step?

Analyzing Step 3.

At this level your sponsee will need to examine A.A. writings about Step 3. To complete this section he/she should read Chapter 5 How it Works up to the bottom of page 63 and Step 3 in the 12 and 12, some questions are added below to guide your teaching.

These questions focus on '**How it Works.**'

1. Many people do recover if they have what?
2. Why do you need to let go of your old ideas?
3. How does this chapter describe alcohol? (This could also be addiction.)
4. What do half measures achieve?
5. What are the 'Steps we took?'
6. What are the three pertinent ideas?
7. What is the first requirement?
8. What are most of us concerned with?
9. If our troubles are of our own making where do they arise from?
10. What do we need to quite playing?
11. Who should you take this step with?
12. What should we do next?

The next questions focus on Step 3 in the **12 and 12**.

13. What is the only key we need?
14. What does Step 3 call for?
15. What have we done without realizing it?
16. Dependence on a higher power seems weak but what do the facts seem to be?
17. Once our independence is in question how do we behave?
18. What might you do if the image in the mirror is too awful?
19. Why can we alcoholics consider ourselves fortunate?
20. List some wrong forms of dependence.
21. How did A.A's cope when World War 2 broke out?
22. How can a willing person continue to turn his will and his life over?
23. Often people are convinced that they should have no self will at all, this is not true. How is this explained in the paragraph beginning 'Then it is explained' (page 41) write a brief summary.
24. So what had our whole trouble been?

Evaluating Step 3.

The task here is to evaluate ideas, judge value, quality or importance and learn to see outcomes that could have been different if your sponsee had not been (or currently is) running on self will.

Some questions to answer could be:

- Select a time when you have made a decision on your own that turned out to be the wrong one. What may have been different if you had listened to others?
- Did you make a decision and still carry it out a decision even though you knew it was wrong? Did your pride or anger not allow you to back down? Was this the right thing to do?
- Are you unwilling to follow direction? Can you follow the suggestions that are being made to you? Do you do this all the time?

Creating with Step 3.

Here your sponsee has to create a list of discussion points that may be discussed with a newcomer that will highlight the problems of running a life on self will. There may be other points that you think you could cover on this step that will be helpful to others, make note of them all.

If you have set a sponsee this task check the discussion points are appropriate before your sponsee talks to newcomers about this step. Make sure that he is ready to complete this part of the learning; you may want to wait until his recovery has been firmly established. If working alone you may wish to check your questions with another person before speaking to others.

Step 4. "Made a searching and fearless moral inventory of ourselves."

Remembering Step 4.

Here we are again, another step to commit to memory. If you find this a bit repetitive that's because it is. Remind your sponsee or your group that this is the first level of learning and forms the bedrock on which all else is built.

Understanding Step 4.

Your sponsee must be able to explain the meaning and idea of Step 4, the crucial next level in learning. Again I suggest reading all of this level before engaging a sponsee.

What does '**searching**' mean?

- To go or look through carefully in order to find something missing or lost.
- To examine carefully in order to find something concealed.
- To explore or examine in order to discover.
- To look at or beneath the superficial aspects of, to discover a motive, reaction, feeling or basic truth.
- To look into, question, or scrutinize.

In Step 4 what is the meaning?

How do we define 'fearless'?

- Oblivious of dangers or perils.
- Calmly resolute in facing fear.
- Possessing or displaying courage.
- Able to face and deal with danger or fear without flinching;

How does the word 'fearless' apply in step 4?

Some explanations of the word 'moral' are:

- Concerned with or relating to human behavior, especially the distinction between good and bad or right and wrong behaviour.
- Adhering to conventionally accepted standards of conduct.
- Based on a sense of right and wrong according to law
- Having psychological rather than tangible effects.

A complex word with many different personal meanings, how does it best apply to this step?

What is an 'inventory'?

- A detailed, itemized list, report, or record of things in one's possession.
- A periodic survey of all goods and materials in stock.
- The process of making such a list, report, or record.
- The items listed in such a report or record.
- An evaluation or a survey of abilities, assets, or resources.

How does this word apply in the context of Step 4?

Now we shall add a little depth to the understanding of these words and the context in which they are meant.

Made a 'searching and fearless'.
Discuss what it means to make a searching and fearless inventory of someones life?

'moral inventory.'
Discuss what a moral inventory is? We know what these words mean individually but what do they mean when combined in this step?

Applying Step 4.

Your sponsee must be able to apply the information learned previously in this step to personal experiences. From what he/she has learned already ask him/her to write some notes on the understanding of Step 4 so far. Here are some headings that may prompt you. The answers should be written.

Give a description of how you could construct a moral inventory. (Not what's in it).

Examine how you feel about this step, does completing a fearless search of yourself give rise to a sense of anxiety, excitement or freedom.

Do you blame others and make excuses for your behavior?

Give an example of your own dishonesty in regards to manipulating or lying to a loved one.

How are the above questions related to Step 4?

Analyzing Step 4.

At this level your sponsee will need to examine A.A.'s writings about taking a moral inventory and compare them to his/her own ideas. To complete this section your sponsee will need to read Chapter 5 How it Works from the bottom of page 63 to the end of the chapter and Step 4 in the 12 and 12. Some questions have been written below to help direct you towards key points.

The first questions are based on Chapter 5.

1. What vigorous course of action should we take and why?
2. So what is Step 4?
3. What does this chapter compare a personal inventory to?
4. Why are we searching out the flaws in our make up?
5. What should be included in our grudge list?
6. What business is infinitely grave?
7. Why is anger a poison to us?
8. How should we react if someone offends us?
9. Why should we put out of our minds the wrongs others had done?
10. What does this chapter say about fear?
11. Read the paragraph on sex, how should we treat this subject?
12. When reviewing your own conduct what should you be looking for?
13. Why should you avoid hysterical thinking or advice?
14. What should you do if sex is very troublesome?

15.If you have been thorough about your personal inventory what will you have achieved?

The next questions focus on Step 4 in the 12 and 12.

16. What do our instincts often far exceed? give examples.
17. What is Step 4 trying to discover?
18. If a person is on the depressive side what is likely to happen when you probe their instincts?
19. What is likely to happen when you investigate someone's instincts who is self righteous or grandiose?
20. What is another excuse for avoiding an inventory?
21. How can a sponsor come to the rescue of these three persons?
22. What are our more glaring personality defects?
23. What conclusion will the newcomer have arrived at?
24. How can a person start a personal inventory, what questions are apt? Write them down.

Evaluating Step 4.

The task here is to evaluate ideas or materials, judge value, quality or importance. Some questions for your sponsee may be;

- Can you think of a better way to clear out the wreckage of the past and perform a personal housecleaning?
- Demonstrate, verbally or in writing, why we should do a moral inventory. Why is it so important?
- Examine the Big Books templates for creating an inventory, why do you think they are laid out in this way? Why do you think people may have re-designed them?
- Evaluate some of your own qualities, which ones do you like, which ones do others like?

Creating with Step 4.

Here your sponsee has to create a Step 4 inventory. Use the same format as in the Big Book unless you have decided on a template you think is better.

Once he/she has created a Step 4 list then create a list of discussion points to help increase the understanding of this Step for newcomers.

If you have set a sponsee this task check the discussion points are appropriate before your sponsee talks to newcomers. Make sure that he/she is ready to complete this part of the learning; you may want to wait until his/her recovery has been firmly established. If working alone you may wish to check your questions with another person before speaking to others.

Step 5. "Admitted to God, to ourselves, and to another human being the exact nature of our wrongs."

Remembering Step 5.

Back to the remembering level again - this first stage of learning and is a must, it is tempting to skip this level or dismiss it as being to much like school.

Understanding Step 5.

To begin the process of understanding this step ask him/ her to look at some of the language used, read the definitions, discuss them and explain them in his/her own words. Remember that first off we are just looking at the words and demonstrating understanding before looking at them in context.

What does the word '**admitted**' mean?

- Confess to be true or to be the case, typically with reluctance.
- Confess to a crime or fault, or one's responsibility for it.
- Accept as valid
- Allow the possibility of.

Some of these explanations are more appropriate than others. Which one best fits Step 5?

How 'exact' is exact? What does it mean? Here are some definitions.

- Not approximated in any way; precise.
- Accurate or correct in all details.
- Tending to be accurate and careful about minor details.

I think all of the above are applicable to this step. Do you?

The word 'nature' has many meanings. What does it mean in this context?

- The basic or inherent features of something.
- The innate or essential qualities or character of a person or animal.
- Inborn or hereditary characteristics of personality.
- A person of a specified character.

What do you understand by the word 'wrongs'?

- Not correct or true
- Unsuitable or undesirable.
- In a bad or abnormal condition; amiss.
- Unjust, dishonest, or immoral.

Which meanings above are your '**wrongs**' closest to?

Drilling down a bit we can discuss these words, and some others in context.

'admitted to'

Discuss what it means to admit to something, are we just admitting? i.e. 'Yeah I did that' or are we making an acknowledgment of past mistakes so as to make a clean start?

'God, ourselves, and another human being'.

There are important reasons for admitting to the above three things, discuss with your sponsee why he/she thinks all three are included. This is covered later when you study the literature about this step so don't worry if your sponsee is not to sure at this stage.

'the exact nature of our wrongs'.

Explain what we mean by 'exact nature', what wrongs are we focussing on? This looks like a small question but the answer can be substantial.

Applying Step 5.

Your sponsee must be able to apply the information learned previously in this step to personal experiences..

Ask him/her to write a short paragraph using the questions below including why they relate to Step 5.

- Write a short piece on why we need the feedback of another person. Do we have the ability to see all the missing pieces of the jigsaw puzzle on our own?
- From what you know of step five write a list of the sort of things we are admitting to. i.e. types of behaviour rather than specific incidences.
- Debate the need to complete a stock take and house cleaning exercise.

Analyzing Step 5.

At this level your sponsee will need to examine A.A.'s writings about step 5 and compare them to his/her own ideas.

To complete this section he/she will need to read Chapter 6 Into Action and Step 6 in the 12 and 12. In order to make the learning process easier a list of questions has again been included to help you focus on certain points within the step.

The below questions focus on **Chapter 6.**

1. What is it we are trying to get and discover?

2. What may people find difficult?

3. What is the 'best reason' for not skipping this step?

4. Why does this chapter compare the alcoholic to an actor?

5. What have we seldom told psychologists (or others)? What has this lead to?

6. What must we be if we want to live long and happily?

7. What guidance does this chapter give to finding the person whom we will share our 5th Step with?

8. What have we no right to do?

9. Why might we postpone this step? What are the dangers of this?

10. What should your chosen partner realize?

11. What should you withhold when you take this step?

12. After sharing this step what does the programme recommend we do?

These questions are on Step 5 in the **12 and 12**

13. Why are few steps harder than Step 5?

14. Why may people try to by-pass Step 5?

15. What has A.A.'s experience taught us about this?

16. Are religions the only advocates of admitting ones defects?

17. What are we likely to receive fromStep 5?
18. What key feelings about forgiveness do we find?
19. What other great dividend may we expect?
20. Why won't a solitary self appraisal be enough?
21. What are the two difficulties of dealing with God ourselves?
22. Why is going it alone in spiritual matters dangerous?
23. What is our next problem?
24. What great moment is apt to occur?
25. What are the real tests of whom you share your self survey with?

Evaluating Step 5.

This level is relatively easy for Step 5 and follows the Big Book to the word. Half way down page 75 starting 'Returning home' are the instructions on how to evaluate what we have done so far. After completing level 6 of Step 5 (the next level) your sponsee is to follow these instructions.

Creating with Step 5.

If working with a sponsee then this is the time to share his/her 4th Step inventory. Remember this does not have to be with you as long as it includes God, himself and another human being. If the sponsee is sharing with you then it is your job to help the sponsee create new understanding and reflection on what has been written.

If it is you who is sharing your inventory then remember the guidance that has been written in the Big Book about whom you share it with.

The next task for your sponsee is to create a list of topic points that may be discussed with newcomers highlighting the key points of Step 5. If you have set a sponsee this task check the discussion points are appropriate before your sponsee talks to newcomers about this step. Make sure that he is ready to complete this part of the learning; you may want to wait until his recovery has been firmly established. If working alone you may wish to check your questions with another person before speaking to others.

Step 6. "Were entirely ready to have God remove all these defects of character."

Remembering Step 6.

Your sponsee must be able to quote Step 6 from memory before moving on to the next level. Learning it from memory does not, at this stage, mean they have to understand it, that is a developing state that takes time and effort. Over the next 5 levels understanding will come. Of course then a sponsee has to live it to really understand - and of course 'give it away' as in the final level of learning.

Understanding Step 6.

Start to explore and then explain the definitions below looking at their context further on in this level.

What does **'entirely'** mean?

- Wholly or fully.
- Completely or unreservedly.
- Solely or exclusively.
- To the full or entire extent.

Step 6 is progressive, as is explored in further levels, does your sponsee think that 'entirely' is do-able?

What does 'remove' mean in the context of Step 6?

- Take something away.
- Eliminate or get rid of.
- Be distant from.
- Be very different from.

If we remove something is it gone permanently, or can we take it back at some time?

Some definitions of 'defects' are;

- A shortcoming or imperfection.
- A failing or deficiency.
- A mark or flaw that spoils the appearance of something.
- Characteristics of an individual that reduce its quality.

Are there any specific defects we are looking for in this step (e.g. the ones that are currently tripping you up)?

What does 'character' mean in this step?

- The mental and moral qualities distinctive to an individual.
- The distinctive nature of something.

- The quality of being individual, typically in an interesting or unusual way.
- Strength and originality in a person's nature.

Ask the sponsee to try and define the two meanings below in their own words.

- 'Were entirely ready to have God remove'.
- 'all these defects of character'.

How do you start to recognise your own defects of character? A list is written at the end of this book to help you think about this.

Applying Step 6.
Your sponsee must be able to apply the information learned previously in this step to personal experiences. From what he/she has learned already ask him/her to write a short paragraph on defects of character and removing them. Some useful headings could also be.

- Describe situations and events where you have been dishonest. What problems has it caused you? What would have been an honest way to have handled the situation?
- Describe situations and events where you have been angry. What problems has it caused you?

What would have been a calm way to have handled the situation?

- Describe situations and events where you have been jealous. What problems has it caused you? What would have been a trusting way to have handled the situation?

Why are these questions applicable to Step 6?

Analyzing Step 6.

At this level your sponsee will need to examine A.A.'s writings about step 6 and compare them to his/her own ideas.

Starting at page 76 ending with the step 7 prayer two paragraphs later ask him/her to read this part of Chapter 6 Into Action. Discuss this short passage. To cover this step in greater depth ask him/her to read Step 6 in the 12 steps and 12 traditions, these questions will help direct you to significant points.

Answer these questions on Step 6 in the 12 and 12.

1. Why is this step the one that separates the men from the boys?
2. What statements are heard daily all over the world?

3. What is it every normal person wants?
4. What happens when we let our natural desires drive us?
5. What are we supposed to be working towards?
6. With what do we need to have patient improvement in?
7. What is the 'best we can do'?
8. If you have escaped the extremes of glaring handicaps can you congratulate yourself?
9. Why can self righteous anger be enjoyable?
10. What is it we prefer to hang on to?
11. Which is the only step that can be practiced with absolute perfection.
12. What should the only question be?
13. So what does that make the other 11 steps?
14. What should we not say to ourselves?
15. Summarise the end of this chapter starting with what happens the moment we say 'no never'.

Evaluating Step 6.

Your sponsee is to consider and examine his/her own defects of character.

A list of personality traits and their opposites are given at the end of the book. You and your sponsee can look at this and perhaps use it as a basis for exploring his/her own defects. In the list is included the opposite of the negative trait so as to give pause for thought on what it is your sponsee could work on to balance out his/her own defects.

Creating with Step 6.

Your sponsee is to create a list of your own character defects in preparation for step 7.

Then your sponsee is to create a list of discussion points that can be talked about with a newcomer that will highlight character defects.

If you have set a sponsee this task check the discussion points are appropriate before your sponsee talks to newcomers about this step. Make sure that he is ready to complete this part of the learning; you may want to wait until his recovery has been firmly established. If working alone you may wish to check your questions with another person before speaking to others.

Step 7. "Humbly asked Him to remove our shortcomings."

Remembering Step 7.
The first task, as per usual, is to learn it parrot fashion, learning it this way of course has many rewards. There may not be many words to this step but there is a lot to work on.

Understanding Step 7.
Your sponsee must be able to explain the meaning and idea of Step 7. To begin the process of understanding this step we will look at some of the language used. To do this ask him/her to read the definitions, discuss them if possible and explain them in his/her own words.

Take a look at different definitions of **'humble'**.

- The quality of being modest.
- Never being arrogant.
- Low in rank, quality, or station.
- An admirable quality that not many people possess. It means that a person may have accomplished a lot but doesn't feel it is necessary to brag about it.
- To cut one's ego down to size.

Explore what the word **'humbly'** means using the definitions above. Does it mean to be subservient and less than? Or could it mean the opposite of arrogance?

Some definitions of **'shortcomings'** are;

- Failure to meet a certain standard.
- A fault or defect.
- Imperfections that detract from the whole.
- The quality or state of being flawed or lacking.

Hmm, I had never thought of being flawed as a quality before. Food for thought.

Putting those words together in Step 7 we get -

'**Humbly** asked Him.'
Discuss this sentence. 'Am I trying to be modest in my request knowing that I want and need help from others'?

'**Remove** our shortcomings.'
Discuss what is meant by the word **'remove'**. Is this permanent or do we need to continue to work on these issues.
Are shortcomings and character defects the same?

Applying Step 7.

Your sponsee must be able to apply the information learned previously in this step to personal experiences. From what he/she has learned already write a short response to the headings below.

- Describe in writing what you think that your life will be like with your defects of character removed from you.
- What defects will be most difficult to give up? Write down why you will find these most difficult.
- What kind of situations or pressure could cause you to regress back into your defects of character? What can you do about it? Summarise your thoughts in a paragraph.

How do these questions relate to Step 7?

Analyzing Step 7.

Again there is little in the Big Book on Step 7 so to cover this in greater depth read Step 7 in the 12 Steps and12 Traditions, some questions are written below to highlight key points.

1. What does Step 7 concern itself with?
2. What is our crippling handicap?

3. What have we never thought of making our daily basis of living?
4. What makes a working faith in a higher power impossible?
5. What can be unbelievably painful?
6. What first milestone do we learn?
7. What inescapable conclusion drives us?
8. What happens after we have taken a square look at some of these defects?
9. What changes in our outlook does this improved perception start?
10. What had been the admission price of a new life?
11. What profound change is the result of learning?
12. What might our deeper objectives be?
13. What is the chief activator of our defects?
14. So what is Step 7 really saying to us?

Evaluating Step 7.

Your sponsee is to make an evaluation of his/her Steps 6 and 7 and decide whether he/she have been forthcoming about his/her defects. Has he/she kept hold of any that he/she is fond of or any that he/she is unwilling to let go.

Creating with Step 7.

Your sponsees next task is to create the right time and environment to complete this phase of Step 7. This is where you and your sponsee will be reading the Step 7 prayer on page 76 in a fashion that best suits his/her personal preferences.

Following this your sponsee should create a list of discussion points that can be talked about with a newcomer that will highlight Step 7. If you have set a sponsee this task check the discussion points are appropriate before your sponsee talks to newcomers about this step. Make sure that he is ready to complete this part of the learning; you may want to wait until his recovery has been firmly established. If working alone you may wish to check your questions with another person before speaking to others.

Step 8. "Made a list of all persons we had harmed, and became willing to make amends to them all."

Remembering Step 8.

Ask your sponsee to learn Step 8 from memory before moving on to the next level.

Understanding Step 8.

Your sponsee must be able to explain the meaning and idea of Step 8. To begin this process some of the words used in this step are identified below and a few definitions to explore are given. Ask your sponsee to read the definitions, discuss them and explain them in his/her own words.

Here are some meanings for '**list**'.

- A series of names or other items written together in a meaningful grouping or sequence so as to constitute a record.
- To set down together in a list.
- Make an index of.

Making a list can simply be that, it does not have to have further information, this will come later.

What do we mean by '**harmed**'?

- Physically injure.
- Damage the health of.
- Have an adverse effect on.
- The act of damaging something or someone.

In the context of the step how may people have been harmed? There is a little more on this later in this section.

What is the meaning of '**willing**'?

- Ready, eager, or prepared to do something
- Of one's own free will.
- Freely and spontaneously.
- Voluntarily or ungrudgingly.
- Of or relating to exercise of the will.

Perhaps a conversation with a sponsee could be centred around the correct application of self will?

Some definitions of '**amends**' could be;

- To correct mistakes made by asking for forgiveness and, or improving the situation that had gone wrong.

- Doing what we can to repair the damage that our past behavior has caused.
- Something done or given by a person to make up for a loss or injury one has caused.
- To change for the better.

There is some depth to understanding the making of amends that is covered in the analyzing section later. A brief discussion about what is meant by amends is all it takes at this level.

Next we shall put each definition in the context of the step.

'Made a **list** of **all** persons we had **harmed**'
You can see from the first part of this step that when put these words together, the task is a lot harder task than perhaps originally perceived. There is a lot more to think about than just the words on their own. Discuss what the first part of the step means and ask your sponsee to describe it in his/her own words.

Ask him/her to explain what is meant by '**all**' persons we had harmed?

'Became **willing** to make **amends** to them all'.

Discuss the following statement - 'The word '**became**' is used because everyone who has attempted this step was unwilling at first to be entirely ready to make that full commitment'.

Is there a reason for using the word '**All**' twice in this step?

Applying Step 8.
Your sponsee must be able to apply the information learned previously in this step to personal experiences. Some topics to write about could be:

- What consequences do you fear in making amends?
- What is the worst thing that can happen? What is the best thing that can happen? What is likely to happen?
- Think of some of the people you have harmed and list the effect on them as individuals and on your relationship.
- Describe any ways that you can use to get rid of the anger and resentment towards anyone on your list.
-

Why do these questions highlight Step 8?

Analyzing Step 8.

At this level your sponsee will need to examine A.A.'s writings about Step 8 and compare them to his/her own ideas.

To complete this section he/she will need to read from the middle of page 76 'Now we need more action' to 'This thought' on page 84. The following questions will give you areas to focus on.

1. What do we need now?
2. What are we trying to repair?
3. On our first approach what need we not do to some people?
4. What should we not do under any condition?
5. What happens in nine cases out of ten?
6. There are some general principles we should follow scattered over the next few pages, what are they?
7. What may you both decide is the way of good sense and loving kindness?
8. Why is the alcoholic like a tornado?

I think it also wise to read the story Freedom from Bondage, in particular the part starting with 'If you have a resentment you want to be free of'. This is only a suggestion that may help some members. It is in the stories section so is not part of the instructions included in the first 164 pages. It does have merit and has worked for many.

The following questions are directed towards Step 8 in the 12 and 12.

9. What are Steps 8 and 9 concerned with?
10. What is a very large order?
11. There are a least four obstacles to Step 8, what are they?
12. As well as making restitution what else is equally necessary?
13. What might we next ask ourselves?
14. What subtler harms may we have committed?
15. What can we now commence to do?
16. What should we avoid?
17. What should this step be the beginning of the end of?

Evaluating Step 8.

At this point your sponsee should re-examine his/her step four inventory for here will be a list of people that will populate his/her Step 8 list. Some people may have destroyed or burned their inventory in some sort of healing ritual and some may have destroyed it in case others find it. Not to worry if your sponsee has, he/she will find their memory is a lot sharper than it has been for a long time and it won't take much to populate a list again. He/she may also find that people needed to be added that weren't in his/her Step 4, this isn't to say that they didn't do a thorough Step 4, just that recovery is progressive and he/she may remember situations differently now from when he/her did their inventory.

Creating with Step 8.

There are now some areas to work on with the list. Study the list of people harmed and form a plan of possible amends for each one of them. Remind your sponsee to always check their thinking with someone else, make sure that he/she doesn't rush headlong into amends that could harm themselves or others.

Your sponsee may wish to prioritise his/her list from easy amends to hard ones, remember that in the Big Book it says that practice will make a person better at making amends, so start with the easy ones. Tell your sponsee not to start making amends until you have completed the work on Step 9.

Your sponsee also have to create a list of discussion points that you can talk about with others that will highlight making amends. If you have set a sponsee this task check the discussion points are appropriate before your sponsee talks to newcomers about this step. Make sure that he is ready to complete this part of the learning; you may want to wait until his recovery has been firmly established. If working alone you may wish to check your questions with another person before speaking to others.

Step 9. "Made direct amends to such people wherever possible, except when to do so would injure them or others."

Remembering Step 9.

Your sponsee must be able to recall Step 9 and recite it back to others from memory. Learning the steps from memory can be very good in reducing feelings of isolation.

Understanding Step 9.

Your sponsee must be able to explain the meaning and idea of step nine. To do this ask him/her to read the definitions given, discuss them and explain them in his/her own words.

What does Step 9 mean by '**direct**'?

- Proceeding without interruption.
- Not deviating or swerving.
- Straightforward and candid.
- Having no intervening persons i.e. do it yourself.
- Consisting of the exact words of the writer or speaker.

In Step 9 how does your sponsee think this applies?

You have covered the meaning of **'amends'** in the previous step but repetition is a key to learning. So what does it mean?

- To correct mistakes made by asking for forgiveness and, or improving the situation that had gone wrong.
- Doing what we can to repair the damage that our past behavior has caused.
- Something done or given by a person to make up for a loss or injury one has caused.

How does your sponsee now regard this word?

'except when' Most people will have no difficulty defining these words, however, because of its importance in this step it is worthy of attention, some of the meanings are;

- Avoiding negative outcomes.
- The task can not be completed unless a condition is met.
- Not under any other circumstance.
- Unless.

Have a short discussion around the meanings here and how they apply.

Again a repetition but time not wasted. What do we mean by **'harmed'**.

- Physically injure.
- Damage the health of.
- Have an adverse effect on.
- The act of damaging something or someone.

Has the sponsee's perception of 'harms' changed at all since the last step?

Below are some meanings for the word **'injure'**.

- Do physical harm or damage to.
- Hurt - Harm - Wound – Impair.
- To cause distress to.
- Wound or injure feelings.
- To commit an injustice or offence against.

Ask your sponsee if all of the above definitions relevant?

Lets put those definitions together in the context of Step 9

Made **'direct amends'**
Discussion point: Why should you make direct amends rather than indirect amends? Is this strictly true?

'**except when** to do so would **injure** them'

Explore the idea that we could 'injure them'. What sort of injuries could we cause?

'**Or others'** Discuss who those others might be.

Before making any amend it is essential that they are discussed with a sponsor first, the harm to others can sometimes be over run by the emotional drive to make all good again.

Applying Step 9.

Your sponsee must be able to apply the information learned previously in this step to personal experiences. Some headings to help could be;

- What amends do you think that you have already made? How have you made them?
- Write a short passage on why you should not make amends in certain circumstances and discuss this with another.
- Take part in some role play with your sponsee or group, get him/her to practice what he/she is going to say when making amends. (Rehearsal can be essential for some people, perhaps the sponsor could play devils advocate or be fantastically over friendly).

Analyzing Step 9.

At this level your sponsee will need to examine A.A. writings about Step 9 and what it means to make direct amends.

These question focus on the latter part of Into Action.

1. What must we take the lead in?
2. To whom should we not talk too incessantly and why?
3. What can we do if there are some wrongs we can never fully right?
4. What are we going to be if we are painstaking about this phase of our development?

The next questions focus on Step 9 in the 12 and 12

5. What qualities shall we need when we take Step nine?
6. What classes can we divide our amends into?
7. When has the process of making amends begun?
8. Why do we only make a general admission of our defects at our first meeting with a family member?
9. What approach should we take at our place of work?
10. What reactions are likely to put us off balance?
11. What great temptation may you face?

12. What is it usually safe to do once you feel confident enough?
13. What one consideration should qualify our desire for complete disclosure?
14. What other razor edged questions may arise in other departments of life?
15. Why should we be absolutely sure we are not delaying?

Evaluating Step 9.

At this point you should sit down and with your sponsee and ask him/her to evaluate the list of amends. Ask him/her to judge the list to see if it is a quality product or whether or not he/she has shied away from some areas. If you are a sponsor it is your job to help with this process, making a judgement as to whether the amends should be made or not, will it harm or heal? Is the timing right?

Creating with Step 9.

Start on the amends. Ask the sponsee to create some discussion points that will help to increase the understanding of Step 9 for a newcomer or any alcoholic that still suffers. If you have set a sponsee this task check the discussion points are appropriate before your sponsee talks to newcomers about this step. Make sure that he is ready to complete this part of the learning; you may want to wait until his recovery has been firmly established.

Step 10. "Continued to take personal inventory and when we were wrong promptly admitted it."

Remembering Step 10.
Your sponsee must be able to recall Step 10 and be able to quote it if asked.

Understanding Step 10.
Your sponsee must be able to explain the meaning and idea of step ten. To begin the process of understanding this step ask him/her to look at some of the language used. Ask the sponsee to read the definitions given, discuss them if possible and explain them in his/her own words.

Some definitions for '**continued**' are:

- Remain in existence or operation.
- Carry on with.
- Keep on working.
- To carry on after an interruption.
- Persist in an activity or process.

Which one is most applicable?

Some of the meanings of '**personal**' are:

- Of, affecting, or belonging to a particular person rather than to anyone else.
- Individual.
- Particular.
- Subjective.

The last definition is a good one in the context of this step and at this stage in recovery should not be a problem.

'**inventory**'. Again we have covered this one, but here is a recap.

- A detailed, itemised list, report, or record of things in one's possession.
- A periodic survey of all goods and materials in stock.
- The process of making such a list, report, or record.
- The items listed in such a report or record.
- An evaluation or a survey of abilities, assets, or resources.

We may all know the definition of 'wrong' but it is worth putting it in the context of Step 10.

'**wrong**'

- Not correct or true.

- Unsuitable or undesirable.
- An unjust, dishonest, or immoral action.
- Act badly toward someone.

How does it fit in with this step?

The word **'promptly'** can be defined as below, which one of the definitions is closer to how it is meant to be understood in Step 10?

- Carried out or performed without delay.
- At once.
- Quick to act as the occasion demands.

For me the last definition is the important one, it allows for time to reflect and pause. Rushing headlong into admitting perceived wrongs could be quite damaging. The saying "A bull in a china shop" could apply.

'admitted' covered already but important none the less important.

- Confess to be true or to be the case, typically with reluctance.
- To permit to enter.
- Acknowledge.
- Accept as valid.

- Allow the possibility of.

Next we shall put each definition into the context of Step 10.

'Continued to take personal inventory'.
We know the meaning of **personal** and **inventory** individually, talk with your sponsee about what they mean together. Discuss with another what it means to take a personal inventory that is continuous.

"and when we were wrong'
Have a talk about knowing when you are wrong. Discuss with your sponsee or another person whether or not it is possible to spot your own wrongdoings all of the time.

Talk with another about the following statement.

- 'It can be worth while setting up a system whereby you check with another person the wisdom of your actions before running headlong into a disastrous amend'.

'Promptly admitted it'
As per previously discussed around the word 'promptly' open up the topic again of how prompt you need to be.

Timing can be important. What are the "it's" were admitting to.

Applying Step 10.

Your sponsee must be able to apply the information learned previously in this step to personal goals.

- Ask the sponsee to construct a plan to allow time for reflection each day?
- Ask him/her to make a list of behaviors or attitudes that he/she will need to guard against in daily living.
- Ask him/her to write a set of self help instructions that he/she can follow if they find themselves in a position that puts them under pressure or they find hard to handle.

If not already working this step prompt your sponsee to start.

Analyzing Step 10.

At this level your sponsee will need to examine A.A. writings about step 10. To complete this section he/she will need to continue to read Into Action starting on page 84 'This thought brings us to step Ten' and also read Step 10 in the 12 and 12.

These first questions focus on Into Action page 84.

1. What is the Step 10 suggestion?
2. So what should our next function be?
3. What is our code?
4. What have we ceased fighting?
5. Why are we neither cocky nor afraid?
6. What is our daily reprieve contingent on?

The following questions will help you study Step 10 in the 12 and 12.

7. What is the acid test?
8. What are necessities for us?
9. What other kind of hangover is there? How do you deal with it?
10. Not all inventories are the same, what distinguishes one from the other and when can they be performed?
11. What is the spiritual axiom that we face?
12. What resentments might we be victimized by?
13. What do we need in all these situations?
14. Why do we look for progress not perfection?
15. Other than disagreeable or unexpected problems what other situations call for self control?
16. What insurance do we have against big shotism?

17. What is it that we begin to see that leads to true tolerance?
18. When we fail somebody what can we do? What are the keynotes that will help us?
19. What should we do at the end of the day?
20. What odd trait of human emotion permeates human affairs from top to bottom?

Evaluating Step 10.

To help assess whether your sponsee is working a good Step 10 consider the questions below.

- Are you continuing to take personal inventory, outline how you do this?
- When you review your day what sort of things are you including?
- Do you struggle with admitting when you are wrong?
- How important is this step? Why?
- Whose guidance do you seek before admitting your wrongs?

Creating with Step 10.

Here your sponsee has to create new discussion points that may be discussed with a newcomer that will highlight the importance of a continued inventory.

If you have set a sponsee this task check the discussion points are appropriate before your sponsee talks to newcomers about this step. Make sure that he is ready to complete this part of the learning; you may want to wait until his recovery has been firmly established. If working alone you may wish to check your questions with another person before speaking to others.

Step 11. "Sought through prayer and meditation to improve our conscious contact with God as we understood him, praying only for knowledge of His will for us and the power to carry that out."

Remembering Step 11.
Your sponsee must be able to recall Step 11 from memory before continuing with the next level.

Understanding Step 11.
Your sponsee must be able to explain the meaning and idea of Step 11. Ask him/her to explore the meanings below, read them, discuss them and explain them in his/her own words.

Some common definitions for '**sought**' are:

- Attempt to find something.
- Attempt or desire to obtain or achieve something.
- Ask for something from someone
- Search for and find someone or something.

It is covered in more depth later but does your sponsee understand the need to seek a new way of living?

We all have an idea of what '**prayer**' means, but what do the books say?

- A religious service, esp. a regular one, at which people gather in order to pray together.
- A solemn request for help or expression of thanks addressed to God or an object of worship.
- An earnest hope or wish .
- The act of making a petition to God, a god, or another object of worship.

Why are we praying? Will it help? How does the sponsee feel about using prayer?

Often a word surrounded with myth and false beliefs, let's have a look at some meanings of **'meditation'**.

- Contemplation of spiritual matters.
- Think intently and at length.
- Reflect deeply on a subject.
- Training the mind to be calm.
- Having one thought at one time.

Those definitions may help your sponsee to see that meditation is not so mystical after all.

Have a look at the meanings of this obvious word **'improve'**:
- To raise to a more desirable or more excellent quality or condition.

- Make better.
- To increase the productivity or value of.
- To put to good use; use profitably.
- To make beneficial additions or changes.

In Step 11 what are we trying to improve?

Examining the definitions above might lead your sponsee to an understanding that change is progressive.

Meanings of **'conscious'** are:

- Aware of and responding to one's surroundings; awake.
- Having knowledge of something.

Both definitions have merit but what do we mean when we use this word in Step 11?

Definitions for **'contact'** are:

- Communicate with typically in order to give or receive specific information.
- Touch.
- Connect with. Coming together of two things.

Some definitions of 'God' are written below below, choose the closest one to your understanding.

- The one Supreme Being, the creator and ruler of t he universe.
- One of several deities, especially a male deity presiding over some portion of worldly affairs.
- A supreme being according to some particular conception.
- Life, Truth, love,
- Mind, Soul, Spirit,
- A Principle.

Again we will cover the meaning of 'understood':
- To perceive the meaning of.
- To be thoroughly familiar with.
- To grasp the significance or importance of.
- To accept as true; believe.
- To accept tolerantly or sympathetically.
- To have knowledge or background, as on a partic ular subject.

Next let's put those words together in the context of the step.
'Sought through **prayer** and **meditation'**

What, when it comes to this step, is it we are seeking?

Talk about prayer with your sponsee or group, discuss morning and evening prayer and the need for praying on an 'as you need it' basis.

Most people to begin with are afraid of meditation and see it as some mystical experience that only the very spiritually enlightened can do. Reassure your sponsee that this is not true and that they will learn more as they progress through this step.

'conscious contact'.
Talk about what it means to have **'conscious contact'** with a higher power and the feelings this may bring. How do you know when you are in contact?

'His will for us' Discuss how you know whose will you are following? You may wish to revisit Step 3 and discuss 'self will run riot'.

'And the **power** to carry that out'A point for discussion could be. God doesn't do things for us directly but gives us the power, if sought, to do those things ourselves.

Applying Step 11.
Your sponsee must be able to apply the information learned previously in this step to personal action.

Ask the sponsee to research different types of meditation techniques, then write a summary of which one best suits their personality. i.e. hypnotherapy CD's, soothing music, candles etc. There are lots of methods out there, find the one that fits. Practice praying. Your sponsee should start to pray as part of a daily routine even if they have no idea who or what their higher power is.

Analyzing Step 11.
At this level you sponsee will need to examine A.A. writings about step 11. He she will need to read the rest of Into Action starting at the bottom of page 85 to the end of the chapter. He/she will also need to read Step 11 in the 12 and 12. In order to make the learning process easier during this section a list of questions has been added below. These will help focus the reader on specific points in each chapter.

The following questions are based on Into Action in the Big book.

1. What is the Step 11 suggestion?
2. What matter should we not be shy on?
3. What should we do when we retire at night?
4. What should you be careful not to drift into?
5. What should we do on awakening?

6. What should we ask God to divorce our thinking from?

7. What should we do when we face indecision?

8. What should we be careful never to pray for?

9. What should we constantly remind ourselves?

10. Because we are undisciplined what should we do?

The next questions are concentrating on Step 11 as written in the 12 and 12

11. How are we apt to regard serious meditation and prayer?

12. Despite all the logic and experience how may newcomers and agnostics view the power of prayer?

13. Why would those of us that have come to make regular use of prayer never do without it?

14. What happens when we link self examination, meditation and prayer?

15. How do you meditate, describe the process?

16. How should beginners in meditation start?

17. What can you do if troubled by intrusive thoughts?

18. What is self forgetting?

19. What is prayer described as? How do you go about it?

20. When we have a decision to make we can pause and say what?
21. What is hazardous about taking a troubling dilemma straight to God?
22. What other temptation can we fall into?
23. What can almost any experienced A.A. tell you?
24. What should you do if seized with a rebellion so sickening that you will not pray?
25. What is one of the greatest rewards of meditation?

Discuss the Serenity Prayer and ask your sponsee to give examples of what this prayer means to him/her.

Evaluating Step 11.

Assess your sponsee's position and understanding of step 11.

Some questions to help with this could be;

- What solution could you apply to improving your meditation?
- When or how often are you praying to your higher power?
- How effective do you think this step is in avoiding relapse?
- Why is this step referred to as a **maintenance** step?

Creating with Step 11.

Your sponsee should have produced some plans and ideas that can help implement this step and now it is time to put them into action and begin working this step on a daily basis.

Again your sponsee should create a list of discussion points that may be spoken about with another that will highlight the key points of Step 11.

If you have set a sponsee this task check the discussion points are appropriate before your sponsee talks to newcomers about this step. Make sure that he is ready to complete this part of the learning; you may want to wait until his recovery has been firmly established. If working alone you may wish to check your questions with another person before speaking to others.

Step 12. 'Having had a spiritual awakening as a result of these steps, we tried to carry this message to alcoholics, and to practice these principles in all our affairs.'

Remembering Step 12.

The final step. The last one to learn off by heart. Remember to ask your sponsee to do this before proceeding.

Understanding Step 12.

Your sponsee must be able to explain the meaning and idea of step twelve. Ask him/her to read the definitions, discuss them and explain them in his/her own words.

First look at **'spiritual awakening'.** There are different ideas as to what these words mean. Have look at some of those ideas.

- A spiritual awakening usually involves a realisation that you are no longer the same.
- A spiritual awakening involves progressive learning.
- A definition in the 12 and 12 says, 'the most important meaning of a spiritual awakening is that a person has now become able to do, feel and believe that which he could not do before'

Discuss the previous definitions and explore what they mean to your sponsee.

Some meanings for **'result'** are:

- A consequence, effect, or outcome of something.
- Occur or follow as a consequence.
- To come about as an end result.

Which meaning fits the meaning in the step?

Look at some of the definitions for the word **'carry'**:

- Take or develop (an idea or activity) to a specified point.
- Move someone or something from one place to another.
- Have on one's person and take with one wherever one goes.

More on this later.

Below are a couple of meanings for the word **'message'**.

- A verbal, written or recorded communication sent to or left for a recipient who cannot be contacted directly.

- A significant point or central theme, especially one that has political, social or moral importance.

Again more later.

A definition of '**alcoholic**' could be:

'An alcoholic is someone who has a primary illness or disorder characterised by loss of control over, and addiction to, the drug alcohol. This causes interference in any major life function, e.g. health, family, job, spiritual, friends and legal'.

Thats a pretty good definition. However we know that it just isn't that simple. Alcoholism is often recognized, by those who have it, to be present whether they are drinking or not.   Discuss with your sponsee his/her interpretation of the word **alcoholic.**

What are '**principles**'? Here are some definitions for you to think over and discuss.

- A fundamental truth or proposition that serves as the foundation for a system of belief or behavior.
- A chain of reasoning.
- A rule or belief governing one's personal behavior.
- Morally correct behavior and attitudes.

What is the meaning of the word '**affairs**' in this context
Do you agree with the two definitions given below?

- An event or sequence of events of a specified kind or that has previously been referred to.
- A matter that is a particular person's concern or responsibility.

Next we shall put each definition into the context of Step 12.

- 'Having had a spiritual **awakening**' Talk about what it means to have had a spiritual awakening. Don't worry about going into to much detail it is covered later.
- 'As a **result** of these steps' What is meant by 'as a result'? a good discussion point could be 'Could I have a spiritual awakening before I complete the steps?
- 'We tried to carry this **message** to **alcoholics**' Talk about the wording of this part of the step. Why does it say '**tried**' instead of leaving this word out?
- What is the **message**?
- Discuss **which** alcoholics we are trying to carry this message to?

- 'Practice these **principles** in all our **affairs'**. Discuss the necessity to work this step in every aspect of your life.

Applying Step 12.

Your sponsee must be able to apply the information learned previously in this step to his/her new life. Here are some headings that may help you do this.

- Discuss the need to continually practice these principles, remembering that we make mistakes and are only human.
- Talk through the following statement. In Step 10 we can promptly admit when our behaviour has been wrong but Step 12 is suggesting that we should keep this behaviour in check, it should no longer get out of place.
- How would you behave in a situation where you felt intimidated or threatened? Why?
- What would you say to someone who is still actively drinking?

Analyzing Step 12.

At this level your sponsee will need to examine A.A. writings about Step 12 and write a breakdown of what the step means. He/she will need to read Working with Others in the Big Book and Step 12 in the 12 and 12.

In order to make the learning process easier during this section a list of questions has been added below. These will help focus the reader on specific points in each chapter. The next questions are focusing on Chapter 7 Working With Others.

1. What has practical experience shown will insure immunity from drinking?
2. What experience must you not miss?
3. What should you do when you discover a prospect for A.A.?
4. What might it be wise to do?
5. When you first meet someone how should this proceed? List the key points.
6. What language had you better use?
7. How do we outline the program of action?
8. What should you make clear?
9. If he is not interested in you solution what may you have to do?
10. How should you proceed if he is sincerely interested?
11. What should be your approach if he thinks he can do the job in some other way?
12. What can you do if your prospect does not respond at once?
13. How should your second visit proceed?
14. What is the foundation stone of your recovery?

15. What idea should be burned into the consciousness of every man?

16. How should you deal with divorce or separation?

17. What can you say to a man who says he can not recover unless he has his family back?

18. If working with a family what should you take care not to do?

19. What can you do assuming you are spiritually fit?

20. What is the rule on avoiding places?

21. Your job now is to be at the place where what?

22. What should you be careful never to show?

23. What do we hope will happen some day?

The following questions are based on Step 12 as written in the 12 and 12.

24. What is the theme of Step 12 What is its key word?

25. Each genuine spiritual awakening has something in common, what is it?

26. What undreamed rewards can helping another alcoholic bring?

27. What does practically ever A.A. member declare?

28. What other kind of Twelfth step work is there?

29. If you find you are unable to speak at meetings what other tasks could you do?

30. How will we come to view setbacks?

31. What is 'the biggest question yet'?

32. What is A.A.'s answer to the questions about living? What are those questions?

33. What is it that the best of us can fall for?

34. How do we cope with basic troubles?

35. After we come into A.A. what happens if we keep on growing?

36. What is the best source of emotional stability?

37. What will your new inner strength and peace enable you to do?

38. What special meaning does A.A. have for those of us who were like that?

39. What has been offset to a surprising extent?

40. What unnatural situations may have developed?

41. After long periods of distortion what may be necessary?

42. Why may the wife (a partner) become discontented?

43. Separation may be necessary but is often uncommon, what usually happens?

44. On the whole what marriages are very good ones?

45. What is likely to occur when "boy meets girl on A.A. campus"?

46. What considerations are equally true and important for those who marry outside of A.A.?

47. What can be said of members who cannot have a family life?

48. What is no longer our principal aim?

49. What may lead us to become victims of unreasonable fears?

50. We found out that freedom from fear was more important than what?

51. What might 'shipwreck' us during our drinking careers?

52. What did we find were willing to stay?

53. So what did the distinguished men have the nerve to say about us?

54. What distorted drives have been restored?

55. What do we find true leadership depends on?

56. To get right with ourselves what do we have to do?

57. Understanding is the key to what?

58. Action is the key to what?

59. What do we hope to sense more deeply with each passing day of our lives?

There is a section in this chapter that summarizes the steps (starting on page 110 with Step 1). Discuss this summary with others or if on your own make some bullet points, or do both.

A Spiritual experience is often mistaken for a spiritual awakening. Read and produce a short summary of 'A spiritual experience' appendix 1 in Alcoholics Anonymous so as to confirm your understanding of the difference.

Evaluating Step 12.

Here your sponsee needs to assess the importance of Step 12 and consider its significance in his/her life. Some questions to answer could be;

- Do you believe that working these steps has significantly improved your life?
- Examining your old behavior, how do you think your life would continue if you failed to maintain the new principles you have learned?
- How important is it to give it away to keep it? What does this mean?
- What's the implication of a 12 step call? How do we do it? What can be the repercussions?
- Why should it be men with men and women with women?
- What is 2 stepping?

Creating with Step 12.

Here your sponsee is to create a list of discussion points that can be talked about with another that will highlight step 12. This will increase his/her own understanding.
If you have set a sponsee this task check the discussion points are appropriate before your sponsee talks to newcomers about this step. Make sure that he is ready to complete this part of the learning; you may want to wait until his recovery has been firmly established. If working alone you may wish to check your questions with another person before speaking to others.

Finally, when having completed the 12 steps your sponsee is to become a sponsor and must apply all this knowledge to educating and nurturing a new sponsee. It is by teaching others that we truly understand what we ourselves have been taught.

Appendix to Step 6.

Aggressive, belligerent - good-natured, gentle

Angry - forgiving, calm, generous

Apathetic - interested, concerned, alert

Apprehensive, afraid - calm, courageous

Argumentative, quarrelsome - agreeable

Arrogant, insolent - unassuming, humble

Attacking, critical - fair, self-restrained

Avoiding - faces problems and acts

Blocking - honest, intuitive

Boastful - modest, humble

Careless - careful, concerned

Cheating - honest

Competitive (socially) - cooperative

Compulsive - free

Conceited, self-important - humble, modest

Contradictory, oppositional - reasonable, agreeable

Contrary, pigheaded - reasonable

Controlling - lets go, esp. of other's lives

Cowardly - brave

Critical - non-judgmental, tolerant

Cynical - open-minded

Deceitful - guileless, honest

Defensive - open to criticism

Defiant, contemptuous - respectful

Denying - honest, accepting

Dependent - accepts help but is self-reliant

Depressed, morose   - hopeful, optimistic, cheerful

Dirty, poor hygiene -clean

Dishonest - honest

Disloyal, treacherous - faithful, loyal

Disobedient - obedient

Disrespectful, insolent - respectful, reverent

Enabling - boundaries, tough love

Envying - empathetic, admiring

Evasive, deceitful - candid, straightforward

Exaggerating - honest, realistic

Faithless, disloyal - reliable, faithful

Falsely modest - honest, has self-esteem

Falsely prideful - modest, humble

Fantasizing, unrealistic - practical, realistic

Fearful - confidant, courageous

Forgetful - responsible

Gluttonous, excessive - moderate

Gossiping - close-mouthed, kind, praising

Greedy - moderate, generous, sharing

Hateful - forgiving, loving, concerned

Hypersensitive - tolerant, doesn't personalize

Ill-tempered, bitchy - good-tempered, calm

Impatient - patient

Impulsive, reckless - consistent, considered actions

Inconsiderate - thoughtful, considerate

Indecisive, timid - firm, decisive

Indifferent, apathetic, aloof - caring

Inflexible, stubborn - open-minded, flexible

Insecure, anxious - self-confident, secure

Insincere, hypocritical - sincere, honest

Intolerant - understanding, patient

Irresponsible, reckless - responsible

Isolating, solitary - sociable, outgoing

Jealous - trusting, generous, admiring

Judgmenta - broadminded, tolerant

Justifying (own actions) - honest, frank, candid

Lack of purpose - purposeful

Lazy, indolent - industrious, conscientious

Loud - tasteful, quiet

Lustful - healthy sexuality

Lying - honest

Manipulative - honest, non-controlling

Masked, closed - honest, open, candid

Nagging - supportive

Narrow minded - open minded

Obscene, crude - modest, courteous

Over emotional - emotionally stable

Perfectionist - realistic goals

Pessimistic - realistic, hopeful, optimistic

Possessive - generous

Prejudiced - open-minded

Procrastinates - disciplined, acts promptly

Projecting (negative) - clear sighted, optimistic

Rationalizing - candid, honest

Resentful, bitter, hateful - forgiving

Resisting growing - willing to grow

Rude, discourteous   - polite, courteous

Sarcastic - praising, tolerant

Self-important - humble, modest

Self-cantered - caring of others

Self-destructive, self-defeating - self-fulfilling

Self-hating - self-accepting, loving

Self-justifying - admitting wrongs, humble

Self-pitying - grateful, realistic, accepting

Self-righteous - humble, understanding

Self-seeking - selfless, concerned for others

Selfish - concerned with others

Shy - outgoing

Slothful (lazy) - industrious, taking actions

Spiteful, malicious - forgiving

Stealing - honest

Stubborn - open-minded, willing

Sullen   - cheerful

Superior, grandiose, pretentious - humble

Superstitious - no magical thinking

Suspicious - trusting

Tense - calm, serene

Thinking negatively - being positive

Treacherous - trustworthy

Undisciplined, self-indulgent - disciplined

Unfair - fair

Unfriendly, hostile, bitchy - friendly

Ungrateful - thankful, grateful

Unkind, mean, malicious, spiteful - kind

Unsupportive of others - supportive

Untrustworthy, unreliable, dishonest - trustworthy

Useless, destructive - helpful, constructive

Vain - modest, humble

Vindictive - forgiving

Violent - gentle

Vulgar - polite

Wasteful - thrifty

Wilful - accepting

Withdrawn - outgoing

Wordy, verbose - frank, to the point, succinct

Bibliography

Alcoholics Anonymous, 3rd edition. New York: Alcoholics Anonymous World Services Inc, 1976. (The 'Big Book.')

Twelve Steps and Twelves Traditions, New York. Alcoholics Anonymous World Services Inc, 1981. (The 'Twelve and Twelve')

Concise Oxford English Dictionary. 12th edition. Oxford University Press Oxford, 2011.

Further word definitions from www.thefreedictionary.com

Anderson, L.W. & Krathwohl, D.R. (Eds.) (2001). A taxonomy for Learning, teaching, and assessing: A revision of Bloom's taxonomy of educational objectives. New York: Addison Wesley Longman.

Geoff Petty, Teaching Today, 3rd edition (2004), Nelson Thornes Ltd, Cheltenham, United Kingdom.

Made in the USA
Las Vegas, NV
06 May 2023

71685094R00066